Nelson Grammar

Pupil Book 1B

OXFORD
UNIVERSITY PRESS

OXFORD
UNIVERSITY PRESS

Great Clarendon Street, Oxford, OX2 6DP, United Kingdom

Oxford University Press is a department of the University of Oxford.
It furthers the University's objective of excellence in research, scholarship,
and education by publishing worldwide. Oxford is a registered trade mark
of Oxford University Press in the UK and in certain other countries

Text © Wendy Wren 2014

Illustrations © Marcus Cutler, Daniel Limon and Elisa Paganelli 2014

The moral rights of the author have been asserted

First published 2014

British Library Cataloguing in Publication Data

Data available

ISBN: 978-1-4085-2388-9

1 3 5 7 9 10 8 6 4 2

Paper used in the production of this book is a natural, recyclable product made from
wood grown in sustainable forests. The manufacturing process conforms to the
environmental regulations of the country of origin.

Printed in Italy by L.E.G.O S.p.A.

Acknowledgements

Series editor: John Jackman
Cover illustrations: Marcus Cutler

Oxford OWL
Discover eBooks, inspirational
resources, advice and support
www.oxfordowl.co.uk

Contents

Naming words

Naming words tell us the names of things.

Naming words are called nouns.

chair

bucket

mat

Focus

A Look at the picture.
How many *naming words* can you find beginning with

1 b   **2** s

B Look at the picture.
Finish the sentences with a *naming word*.

1 The dog is digging in the _____ .

2 The boy is making a _____ .

3 Dad is eating a _____ .

4 The baby is asleep in the _____ .

5 There is a boat on the _____ .

6 They are playing with a _____ .

7 The _____ is shining.

8 The dog has found a _____ .

9 Dad is sitting on a _____ .

10 The baby is under the _____ .

A **sentence** starts with a **capital letter**.

A **sentence** usually ends with a **full stop**.

These are **telling** sentences.

They are **statements**.

My name is Tom**.**

These sentences
tell us something.

Some **sentences** end with a **question mark**.

These are **asking** sentences. They are **questions**.

What is your name**?**

These sentences
ask us something.

Focus

A Look at the picture.

1 Say the **telling sentences**.

2 Say the **asking sentences**.

B *Ask* Tom about:

1 his hair

2 his height

3 his brothers and sisters

4 his pets

C *Tell* Kim about:

1 your favourite subject

2 your last name

3 the sport you like

4 your favourite book

Doing words

1

My name is Eva.
I am flying a kite.

2

This is Tom.
He is swimming.

3

Here is Nadia.
She is feeding the dog.

4

The dog is called Jack.
Jack is eating.

5

We are twins.
We are doing sums.

6

The cats are Bill and Ben.
They are sleeping.

Am, is and are help to make doing words.

Doing words are called **verbs**.

am, is, are	+ verb family name	+ ing
I **am** looking.	I **am** painting.	I **am** washing.
He **is** walking.	She **is** talking.	It **is** drinking.
You **are** working.	They **are** laughing.	We **are** playing.

Focus

A Look at the pictures.
Say what they are *doing*.

1 What is Eva doing?   2 What is Tom doing?

3 What is Nadia doing?   4 What is Jack doing?

5 What are the twins doing?   6 What are the cats doing?

B Choose *am*, *is* or *are*.

1

The cats _____ playing.

2

She _____ riding.

3

Tom _____ running.

4

Jack _____ digging.

Special naming words

This is Y1.

Mrs Hill is their teacher.

This is Y1's timetable.

Monday	English	Maths	B	PE	Music	L	Spelling	B	Story time
Tuesday	Maths	English	R	Art	Reading	U	Story time	R	PE
Wednesday	Art	English	E	Reading	Music	N	Maths	E	Story time
Thursday	English	Music	A	Art	Reading	C	PE	A	Story time
Friday	Maths	Art	K	English	Music	H	Reading	K	PE

Special naming words have capital letters.

Names of people are special naming words.

    Mrs Hill

Days of the week are also special naming words.

    Monday   Tuesday

Special naming words are proper nouns.

Focus

A Look at the timetable.
Read the *days of the week*.

B Look at the timetable.
Answer the questions.

  1 When is English the first lesson?

  2 When is Maths the first lesson?

  3 When is Story time the last lesson?

  4 When is PE the last lesson?

C Answer the questions.

  1 What is the first day of the school week?

  2 What is the last day of the school week?

  3 What are the two days at the weekend?

D Which day begins with the letter:

  1 F   **2** M

E Which days begin with the letter:

  1 T   **2** W

A **sentence** starts with a **capital letter**.

A **sentence** usually ends with a **full stop**.

These are **telling sentences**. They are **statements**.

    I am going by train.

Telling sentences can also be called **commands**.

    Wait for me!

Some sentences end with a **question mark**.

These are asking sentences. They are **questions**.

    What time is your train?

Some sentences show people are:

    shouting   angry   surprised

HELP!

GO AWAY!

WOW!

These sentences end with an **exclamation mark**.

They are **exclamations**.

    I have missed my train!

Capital letters, full stops, question marks and exclamation marks are all **punctuation marks**.

Focus

Look at the picture. Find:

1 a telling sentence   •

2 an asking sentence   **?**

3 an exclamation   **!**

Describing words

❶ tall

❷ small

❸ fat

❹ thin

❺ little

❻ big

❼ long

❽ short

❾ wide

❿ narrow

⓫ cold

⓬ hot

⓭ wet

⓮ dry

⓯ young

⓰ old

Describing words are called **adjectives**.

They tell us more about people, places and things.

a **round** ball

a **pretty** flower

a **happy** child

Focus

A Look at the pictures.
Read the *describing words*.

B Say a sentence for each picture.
Say the *describing words*.

The first one is done for you.

1 Number 1 is a tall man.

2 Number 2 is a _____ _____.

3 Number 3 is a _____ _____.

4 Number 4 is a _____ _____.

5 Number 5 is a _____ _____.

6 Number 6 is a _____ _____.

7 Number 7 is a _____ _____.

8 Number 8 is a _____ _____.

9 Number 9 is a _____ _____.

10 Number 10 is a _____ _____.

11 Number 11 is a _____ _____.

12 Number 12 is a _____ _____.

13 Number 13 is a _____ _____.

14 Number 14 is a _____ _____.

15 Number 15 is a _____ _____.

16 Number 16 is a _____ _____.

1

Special naming words

January

February

March

April

May

June

July

August

September

October

November

December

Special naming words have capital letters.

Names are special naming words.

    Mrs Hill

Days of the week are special naming words.

    Monday

Months of the year are also special naming words.

    January

Focus

A Look at the pictures. Read the *months of the year*.

B Look at the pictures. Answer the questions.

  1 Which month has snow?

  2 Which month has yellow flowers?

  3 When can you see lambs?

  4 Which month has leaves falling?

  5 When is Bonfire Night?

C Answer the questions.

  1 What is the first month of the year?

  2 What is the last month of the year?

  3 What is the month of your birthday?

D Which months begin with:

  1 D   **2** F   **3** O

  4 N   **5** S

E Which months begin with:

  1 A   **2** J   **3** M

Doing words

1

prowl**ed**

2

watch**ed**

3

walk**ed**

4

lift**ed**

5

chew**ed**

6

jump**ed**

The words in the pictures are **doing words**.
They are called **verbs**.
They tell us what people, animals and things **did** in the past.

help**ed**   peck**ed**   talk**ed**

verb family name + **ed**

        help + ed = help**ed**

        peck + ed = peck**ed**

        talk + ed = talk**ed**

Focus

A Look at the pictures.

    Tell the story.

B Answer the questions.

Picture **1** What did the lion do?

Picture **2** What did the hunter do?

Picture **3** What did the lion do?

Picture **4** What did the net do?

Picture **5** What did the mouse do?

Picture **6** What did the lion do?

Use the **doing word** under each picture.

More than one

We add **s** to **naming words** when we mean **more than one**.

 One is **singular**. More than one is **plural**.

one hat

two hat**s**

If a **naming word** ends in **ch sh s** or **x** we add **es**.

one match

six match**es**

Focus

A Look at the picture. Say how many.

1 glass   2 bus   3 watch

4 box   5 dress   6 torch

B Do these word sums.

1 glass + es =

2 bus + es =

3 watch + es =

4 box + es =

5 dress + es =

6 torch + es =

We use **joining words** to **join sentences**.

A useful **joining** word is **and**.

Sentence 1:   Mum made a cake.

Sentence 2:   She put it in the oven.

You can make one sentence by using *and*.

You need **one** capital letter and **one** full stop.

Mum made a cake **and** she put it in the oven**.**

Focus

Look at the pictures.

1 What is happening in picture 1a?

What is happening in picture 1b?

Say what is happening in 1a and 1b.   Use **and**.

2 What is happening in picture 2a?

What is happening in picture 2b?

Say what is happening in 2a and 2b.   Use **and**.

3 What is happening in picture 3a?

What is happening in picture 3b?

Say what is happening in 3a and 3b.   Use **and**.

Special naming words

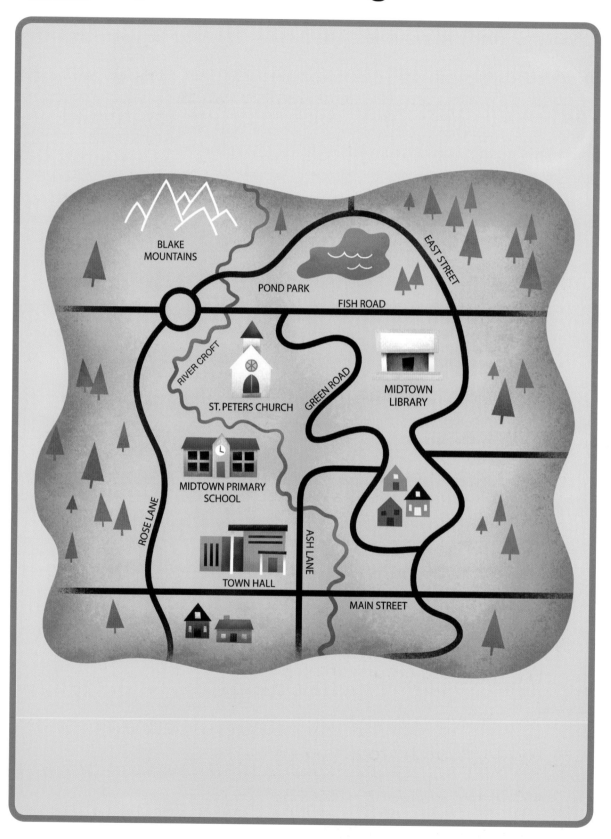

BLAKE MOUNTAINS

POND PARK

FISH ROAD

EAST STREET

RIVER CROFT

ST. PETERS CHURCH

GREEN ROAD

MIDTOWN LIBRARY

MIDTOWN PRIMARY SCHOOL

ROSE LANE

ASH LANE

TOWN HALL

MAIN STREET

Special naming words have capital letters.

Names are special naming words.

   Mrs Hill

Days of the week are special naming words.

   Monday

Months of the year are special naming words.

   January

Names of places are also special naming words.

   Midtown

Focus

A Look at the map. Read the *place names*.

B Look at the map. Answer the questions.

   1 What is the name of the town?

   2 What is the name of the school?

   3 What is the name of the church?

   4 What is the river called?

   5 What is the park called?

   6 What are the mountains called?

C Do you know…

   1 the name of the road you live in?

   2 the name of the town you live in?

   3 the name of your school?

Doing words

walked

pointed

touched

crashed

shouted

walked

The words in the picture are **doing words**.

They are called **verbs**.

Verbs tell us what people, animals and things **did**.

chew**ed**   play**ed**   jump**ed**

verb family name + **ed**

    chew + ed = chew**ed**

    play + ed = play**ed**

    jump + ed = jump**ed**

Focus

A Look at the pictures.

   Tell the story.

> Use the **doing word** under each picture.

B Answer the questions.

   Picture **1** What did the class do?

   Picture **2** What did the teacher do?

   Picture **3** What did the boy do?

   Picture **4** What did the shield do?

   Picture **5** What did the manager do?

   Picture **6** What did the boy do?

1
a happy

b **un**happy

2
a tidy

b **un**tidy

3
a friendly

b **un**friendly

4
a successful

b **un**successful

Describing words are called **adjectives**.

Adjectives can have **opposites**.

un + describing word = opposite

lucky

unlucky

 Look at the pictures.

Read the *describing words*.

Read the *opposites*.

B Finish and say the sentences.

1 Picture **①** **a**   It is a _____ face.

Picture **①** **b**   It is an _____ face.

2 Picture **②** **a**   It is a _____ room.

Picture **②** **b**   It is an _____ room.

3 Picture **③** **a**   The man is _____ .

Picture **③** **b**   The man is _____ .

4 Picture **④** **a**   The girl is _____ .

Picture **④** **b**   The boy is _____ .

UNIT 14 Naming words

Naming words tell us the names of things.

Naming words are called nouns.

bicycle   car

We can make naming words from doing words.

doing word	naming word
paint	painter

Focus

A Look at the picture.
Complete the sentences.

The first one has been done for you.

1 Can you see the girl **riding**?   She is a rider.

2 Can you see the man **cleaning** the windows?   He is a _____ .

3 Look at the lady **shopping**.   She is a _____ .

4 There is a man **driving**.   He is a _____ .

5 Can you see the man **sweeping** the road?   He is a _____ .

B What are you if you:

1 swim a _____   2 sing a _____

3 build a _____   4 bake a _____

31

How to use this book

The heading tells you what the page is about.

This box gives you information about different types of words and sentences.

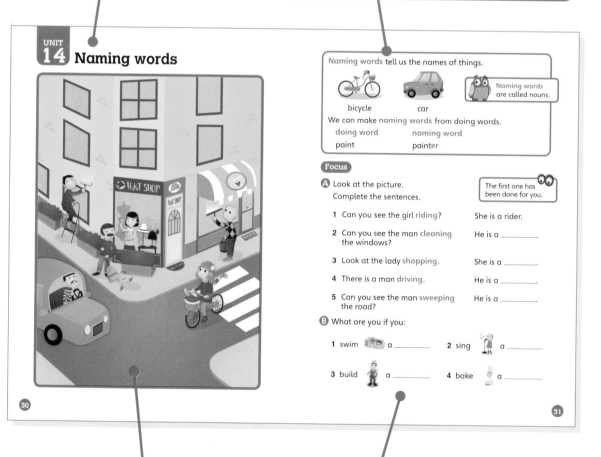

Look at the picture and talk about it.

Talk about these questions before you answer them.